ALEXIS' ISLAND

GROWING UP IN THE TROPICAL PARADISE OF KEY WEST

by

David L. Hemmel and Janette C. Knutson

Duval Publishing
Key West, Florida

Publisher's Cataloging-in-Publication
(Provided by Quality Books, Inc.)

Hemmel, David L.
    Alexis' island : growing up in the tropical paradise
of Key West / by David L. Hemmel and Janette C. Knutson.
        p. cm.
        SUMMARY: Describes the everyday life of a boy living
aboard ship at America's southernmost island, Key West,
including such topics as history of the region, marine
environment, sailing, and local characters.
        Audience: Ages 8-18.
        ISBN 0-9745637-2-2

    1. Key West (Fla.)--History--Juvenile literature. 2.
D'Albissin, Alexis Girard. 3. Children--Florida--Key
West--Social life and customs--Juvenile literature. 4.
Boat living--Juvenile literature. 5. Marine biology--
Florida--Key West--Juvenile literature. [1. Key West
(Fla.)--History. 2. D'Albissin, Alexis Girard. 3. Key
West (Fla.)--Social life and customs. 4. Boat living.
5. Marine biology.]   I. Knutson, Janette C. II. Title.

F319.K4H46 2006   975.9'41
                             QBI06-600129

Duval Publishing
P. O. Box 4255
Key West, Florida 33041
Tel: 1/305-292-6465

A Special Thank You

Alexis is an exceptional boy with a generous heart who has inspired us with his patience and humility. Portraying Key West in terms of his world would not have been possible without the understanding of his sister, Clementine, and the trust and cooperation of his parents, Naja and Arnaud. It has been a privilege to be invited into a family that nurtures respect for themselves and others, develops a relationship with, and a reverence for their environment, gives wing to their creativity, and demonstrates how to deal with the surprises, both good and bad, of living.

Several other members of the harbor community have been gracious and helpful in the preparation of "Alexis' Island". Don Kincaid has been an invaluable source on the Atocha discovery days as well as many other facts from his "growing up" in Key West. He is also a supurb photographer whose works appear in this book. Lobster Lee shared insights into the life of those making a living harvesting from the sea as well as interesting facts on lobster and shrimp. Claudia Pennington generously allowed the reproduction of one of the Custom House's Mario Sanchez prints. Captain Victoria shared her extensive knowledge of dolphins. Cory Malcom of the Mel Fisher Museum provided valuable help on Atocha artifacts.

We are also indebted to Tom Hambright of the Monroe County Library; Peter Anderson, Kate Milano, and the Fairy Princess of the Conch Republic; Captain Jay Weed and his Lucky fleet; Tom Matthews of the Marine Research Institute, Marathon; Reef Relief; June Keith; Ed Little; and Howard Phoenix.

Island Ventures

1. Living Aboard

Gaspard
The Spare House

Coco Loco
The Main House

Alexis' home sits in a harbor just across from Key West in the state of Florida. A mere dot in the Atlantic Ocean, this island paradise is the most southern point in the United States. Here, Mile Marker Zero begins the measure of miles north along the eastern coast. For this reason it is often referred to as the end of the road.

Interestingly though, the end of the road is often the beginning of the road for those who come here in search of something they don't already have.

Alexis' father, Arnaud, came to Key West from France. His mother, Naja, came from New York. Both were attracted by life on the water, the climate and the small size of the community.

Arnaud

Alexis helps out with salvage work

Alexis and his sister, Clementine, were born on a sixty four foot sailboat named Gaspard. Gaspard has one bedroom, which sailors call a cabin, a bathroom, which sailors call the head, and a kitchen, which sailors call a galley.

The family and their two year old cat, Shookey, now live on Coco Loco, a seventy nine foot former luxury yacht. Coco Loco has nine cabins, three heads and a galley.

Gaspard has become Arnaud's

workshop. This is where he repairs engines and welds broken parts for other boaters. The whole family crams onboard Gaspard when Arnaud is working on Coco Loco. Everyone looks forward to the day when the renovations are finished and Coco Loco is restored to its former beauty. Then they will have lots of room for sleep overs.

Every morning Alexis wakes to the sound of seagulls chattering in the new day as they go about their morning scavenge. He may be lucky enough to see a graceful split tail frigate dive into the ocean for the breakfast his keen eyes have spied from hundreds of feet above the water.

Every night he closes his eyes to the bright, shining stars that twinkle above and the lights that glitter and sparkle in Key West. Now and then an osprey, a highly skilled fisherman, lands on the mast of Alexis' floating home and bids him good night.

Both day and night, the ocean breezes create gentle waves that continuously lap his world. When a tropical storm evolves into a hurricane, however, life onboard becomes uncomfortable and dangerous. As the waves churn and roll the boats from one side to the other, what was peaceful and calm becomes a

Climbing the sailboat's boom and mast with friends

Chart tables can be used for plotting courses at sea or for homework.

battlefield for
survival.

On calm days, dolphins may swim by
their boat inviting Alexis and Clementine
to jump into their aqua playground.
Barracuda, jacks, yellow and black striped
sergeant majors, yellow tails, and grunts
know they are welcome guests to the
scraps thrown overboard after dinner.

Other vessels, like weather beaten
houseboats and sailboats, with and

without masts,
float around Alexis'
home. Together they form a
supportive network where adults look out
for each other and truly believe that the
community raises the child.

Each vessel has a dinghy attached to it. A
dinghy is a small boat with a motor sort

of like a family car for running errands on water. The dinghy allows people who live on the anchorage to go to Key West to shop, haul water and get to places like school. It also allows friends who live aboard to visit each other and to travel to islands where they can explore.

When not in use, the dinghy is tied to the main boat's stern by a short rope called a painter. While planing over the water, some people hold onto the painter and balance with their legs. This enables them to have a smoother ride and to stay dry.

Several islands around Alexis' home form an extended community just like the suburbs that make up a city on land. These islands are called Keys.

Over the railing, grunts wait for a free meal.

Key West

During the 1960's, the Navy dredged Key West Harbor so it could steer vessels safely through the shallow waters. The substance they dredged from the sea floor is a crumbly, earthy mixture of clay and calcium carbonate called marl. The navy piled the marl into mounds and formed man made islands. Christmas Tree, formally known as Wisteria Island, and Sunset Key, actually named Tank Island, as well as parts of Stock Island, were formed this way.

Other islands in the area were formed naturally when coral deposits were exposed over time as the depth of the

(or Cayo Hueso to its Spanish neighbors)

sea lowered. After many years, these islands became home to mangroves.

Mangroves are very important. They are a nesting ground for birds and a nursery for fish. They keep the water clean by trapping debris and filtering harmful chemicals released by boats and industry. Also, mangroves create a buffer from hurricanes.

The nautical charts name over eight hundred Keys. Many others are still as yet unnamed.

The main Keys are connected to each other and the mainland by bridges. Some Keys, not subject to the constant traffic created by these bridges, remain cut off and more private, accessible only by boat.

Key West

Key West is the main island suburb in Alexis' city on the water. It is protected from the sea by a beautiful coral reef that lies about seven miles out. The Spanish named it Cayo Hueso, which means Bone Island, after finding it covered with bones left behind from a battle between Indian tribes.

Since an estimated one and a half million tourists per year arrive in Key West, on cruise ships, in recreational boats and in cars, the island has many restaurants offering exotic seafood and other delicacies from a variety of cultures, especially Cuban.

Alexis chats with a friend on famous Duval Street.

Music on the island ranges anywhere from rock to jazz to symphony to salsa and is as diverse and delightful as the food.

Many of the establishments that provide such fine food and music are found on Duval Street. This is also where tourists can find novelty stores offering a range of goods from T-shirts for as low as five dollars to rare treasures that may have lain on the ocean

Colorful roosters, hens and their chicks come and go as they please.

floor for four centuries. Depending on whether the treasure is a single coin or a clump, an emerald, pearl or gold chain, it can sell for hundreds to tens of thousands of dollars.

Museums on the island document its history and tell stories of discovering treasure, salvaging shipwrecks, pirates, slave ships, early settlers, customs and industry.

Roosters roam free, with their family of mother hen and chicks looking for food. They have beautiful iridescent, green, brown, red, and gold feathers. The hens are less colorful so they don't attract attention when they are nesting.

Their ancestors' owners kept them in cages where they lived and laid their eggs. Sometimes they were made to claw each other in cock fights where men bet money on which rooster would win. Today, they don't belong to anyone.

Residents and visitors like to see them pecking in gardens and yards. Sometimes they feed them, but this is discouraged.

Roosters herald both the dawning and closing of day, but they can wake up residents with their "cock-a-doodle-doo" anytime during the night. Recently the city hired a man to round them up. Overall, it wasn't a popular idea, and the man eventually lost interest in the job.

Cats, both tame and wild, are other famous inhabitants of Key West. Some concerned citizens ride their bikes around at night putting out food and looking for abandoned kittens.

Key West is also home to many dogs of varied personalities, including Dick the Dog who dresses as Uncle Sam for a celebration called Fantasy Fest. This big dress up party occurs during the last week of October.

mane and tail to look just like a lion.

A popular event is the Pet Masquerade. Owners dress their pets and enter them in a competition for best dressed and most entertaining. Often the owners are similarly dressed, or, they compliment their dogs in what they wear.

This year a dog and her owner dressed as witches while another owner dressed her dog as an astronaut and herself as an alien. One dog had his fur trimmed with a

Look alikes in the Pet Masquerade

Christmas Tree Island

Christmas Tree Island

The closest island to Alexis' boat and home is Christmas Tree, a small island to the east with lots of trees and washed up boat wrecks. Sometimes Alexis and his friends camp out there. Last

Christmas was particularly fun when their neighborhood spent Christmas Eve on the island decorating trees and Christmas Day exchanging gifts. It would also be a great place for an Easter egg hunt.

Do You Know Where Salt Comes From?

The grocery store, of course. But where is it made and how? Well, in old Key West, settlers knew they could not survive without salt. It was needed to preserve food on a tropical island where ice was not too plentiful. So they built salt ponds to extract the salt they needed from the ocean all around them.

These ponds, shown above, were shallow pools that were excavated with canals connecting them to the ocean.

At high tide, the ocean flowed in and filled the ponds. The gates were then closed, and the water evaporated leaving only the salt. This was repeated several times until the salt became quite thick and could be shovelled into bags.

Today, the salt ponds are beautiful wildlife areas where kayakers can see egrets and herons wading along the mangrove lined shores.

Split Rock Key

Split Rock Key

Split Rock Key is one of those unnamed Keys in the nautical charts. Some locals refer to it as Split Rock Key while others refer to it as Destroyer Key. How it became split in two is questionable. Some believe a Navy destroyer ran aground while others believe it was a treasure

hunter. According to one local resident, the real story is that two destroyer escorts ran aground during a hurricane in 1947. To get them out, the Navy dredged a channel and piled the marl on either side. Whether it was a destroyer, its escorts or a treasure hunter that split the island doesn't really matter. But you can see how it came to be referred to by its two names. When officials create the

Relaxing after a swim

next nautical chart for the area, they will probably take a consensus. On that basis, it will officially be named Split Rock or Destroyer Key. On the other hand, they may come up with an entirely new name, or they may combine the names and call it something like Destroyer Rock. Whether you call it Split Rock or Destroyer Key, it is a great place to picnic and explore. This is where Alexis and Clementine learned to swim.

Boca Grande is an inviting tropical island ...

Boca Grande

A visit to Boca Grande is like a visit to your very own private beach or park. Alexis' mom packs a picnic lunch, and off the family goes in one of their smaller boats.

Boca Grande has a beautiful white sandy beach where Alexis and Clementine often find interesting and perfectly formed shells. It is a natural island that was not created

16

... with hidden ponds, cormorants, and sandy beaches

through dredging. A swim in the blue green waters refreshes them on a hot and humid summer day. In this ocean swimming pool, they may run into a ray as it glides, leaps and dives, or a turtle, as it paddles along. They also love to climb the mangrove trees that grow on the island and explore their intricate root systems.

17

First mate Alexis secures the family water taxi to the dock.

Alexis' mother and father are boat captains. They own and operate the water taxi that transports boaters to and from Key West.

They also salvage boats that have been destroyed and washed ashore by storms and the hurricanes that make their unwelcome summer visits. Alexis is too young to help with some of the heavy work of salvaging, but he can help with the water taxi business. Although he cannot yet steer the taxi, he can secure the boat by tying a rope to the piling on the

The artist is put in charge of making signs for the boat.

Alexis earns spending money by selling his books and inventions to curious customers at the Blue Heaven Restaurant.

dock when it reaches the marina. He is also able to untie the rope before leaping aboard when his mother is ready to leave.

Alexis helped prepare the water taxi for business by tracing a stencil of the logo onto each side of the boat.

He spends Sundays at an outdoor restaurant in Bahama Village called Blue Heaven. It is crowded with tourists and locals eating delicious meals on gray, sun dried, wooden tables, benches and chairs. The sand covered ground suggests you are somewhere by the beach and life is uncomplicated. Roosters and chickens run around between the tables. Waiters and waitresses dart meals, coffee pots and empty plates from the kitchen to the tables and back again. A band plays. Their music is soulful and brings back memories and feelings for those old enough to remember. Songs by Louis Armstrong like "It's a Wonderful World" and a sad ballad about returning to Jamaica that makes you want to go too.

Alexis pays five dollars a week to rent his space at Blue Heaven where he sits at two card tables. An umbrella clamped to one of the tables protects him from the harsh rays of an endlessly brilliant sun. On the tables are copies of his book of poetry titled "The Worshiped Island," which he sells for ten dollars, and, his latest invention, a magic trick. It is a recycled liquid soap bottle decorated with bright images. When he raises his hand, the object inside moves

up. When he lowers his hand, it moves down. Although he won't tell customers exactly how his magic power works, he hints that it has something to do with squeezing the bottle.

It is not uncommon for Alexis to make seventy five dollars in three hours. By the end of the morning, he is ready for lunch.

The Gumbo Limbo tree invites him to cool off under its generous branches. There he enjoys the fried chicken, grapes and orange juice Naja and Clementine bring back from Fausto's Food Palace. Later on he will sip the milk from a coconut. At the end of the day, Alexis is ready for a well earned break. He may just decide to go sailing.

Arnaud has taught his son much about sailing. Alexis refines his technique during the summer sailing classes he takes with other children.

He knows how to catch the wind in order to set his sail. He knows how to handle the rudder so he can steer the boat exactly where he wants to go. He knows how to navigate. He has mastered the rules of the road to avoid colliding with another boat.

"I like that you can do something by yourself," Alexis says.

"You have to think to survive. You have to make sure the boat doesn't sink."

Until he learned how to jibe in sailing classes, Alexis tipped his boat every time he went out.

"Jibing is for going downwind. Tacking is for going upwind," he explains. "The boom holds the sail down on the bottom. You hold on to the main sheet to control the sail. You can let go if you're going downwind."

He has fun playing with the

wind and the water. It's kind of like a solitary board game of survival. The water is the board along which his sailboat glides. The wind is the dice that allows him to move and change direction. Jibing and tacking involve tricky maneuvers that require thought like outwitting an enemy. Alexis is the player who controls where and how fast he wants to go on his journey of discovery.

"You have to think to survive"

The children who were born in the early days of Key West didn't have cars, bicycles or powerboats. If they wanted to go fishing or explore neighboring islands, they needed to find an old wooden boat. A neighbor may have given them one he no longer needed. Sometimes their father or their grandfather helped them build one.

If they were lucky enough to get possession of a boat, their mother would sew a sail from heavy canvas. With a wooden mast, some ropes for a halyard,

When Alexis learned to sail, he also learned to tie knots.

How to Tie Sailor Knots

The Bowline

This is the most useful knot on a sailboat. It is strong, won't slip, and, most importantly, can be easily untied in an emergency no matter how tight the wind has pulled it.

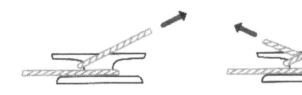 

Tying Your Boat to a Cleat

If you want your boat to be where you left it when you return the next morning, it's important to tie it correctly to the dock cleat.

How a Sailboat Works

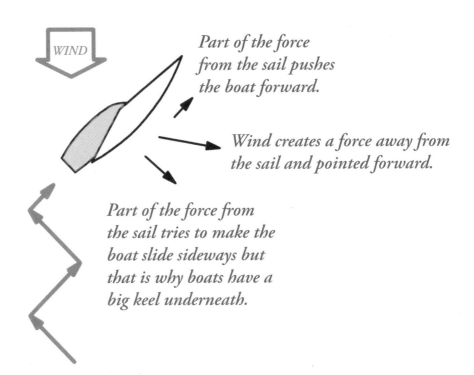

WIND

Part of the force from the sail pushes the boat forward.

Wind creates a force away from the sail and pointed forward.

Part of the force from the sail tries to make the boat slide sideways but that is why boats have a big keel underneath.

Boat must tack back and forth to move forward against the wind.

which are the ropes you pull the sail up with, and sheets, which are the ropes you pull the sails in and out with, they had a small boat for exploring. Now they could visit deserted beaches and look for turtle eggs, find old Indian pottery that once belonged to the very first settlers, or take some conch home for dinner.

Their fathers taught them how to set the

sails perfectly to get the most speed and how to tack and jibe. They taught them how to tie a bowline and a clove hitch, how to braid a rope to make a round hoop, or eye, in the end, and, how to splice two lines together.

They taught them where to safely drop the anchor so it would hold and not drag over the sand, coral or seaweed on the ocean floor. They also taught them how much anchor line to put out.

They taught them how to read the weather and when to dash back to shore if a bad storm was approaching.

Sailing off to another adventure or to catch dinner for mom?

Most importantly, they taught them how to read the color of the water so they could tell how deep it was

and what was on the bottom of the ocean.

One day Alexis will sail off on a brand new adventure in the sailboat he and Arnaud are rebuilding from used parts. In the meantime he will develop his skills by sailing over to nearby Christmas Tree Island and, eventually, to Boca Grande.

In addition to just plain exploring, sailing is a way to see all the birds and sea creatures around the islands. Pelicans and gulls fish busily around him. A turtle may surprise him when it pokes its head up to look around. Playful dolphins may decide to accompany him, sometimes swimming alongside his boat.

5. Ocean Friends

There are forty species of dolphin in the world. They live in family groupings called pods. The Coastal Atlantic Bottlenose species lives in and around the waters of Key West.

Dolphins communicate with each other using signals that are similar to the sound of human voices singing. When Alexis and Clementine sing, they are recognized by their dolphin friends. Sometimes they tease Alexis and Clementine by swimming up close. Then they dive underneath them before coming up in a splashing surprise on the other side.

... dolphins are our kind and caring friends in treacherous and hostile seas.

It is believed that dolphins are good friends of humans and can cure them of their illnesses. That's why people who are sick, or who have disabilities, often seek them out. Even if dolphins don't make them better, they comfort their human friends by making them feel they are accepted exactly as they are.

29

The Greeks offered an explanation for dolphins' affinity to humans. According to ancient Greek mythology, pirates once captured Dionysus, the god of wine and peace. They did not know he was a god. Instead, they thought he was a strong, young man they could sell as a slave, or, a person of wealth they could ransom. At first Dionysus was amused by their antics but when they refused to let him go he became annoyed. Since they loved wine he decided to cover their ship in vines ladened with grapes. The pirates had no choice but to jump overboard to escape the terrifying sight before them. Rather than let them drown, Dionysus turned them into dolphins. Although there are many myths about how they came to be, all agree that dolphins are our kind and caring friends in treacherous and hostile seas.

At night Alexis can look up from his boat and see the Dolphin constellation to the right of the Mlky Way. He wonders if his ocean friends are also about to go to sleep or if they will be up playing all night.

Alexis and a friend watch Key West lobstermen at work.

Dolphin share the waters around Key West with a rich medley of marvellous creatures. Lobster, shrimp, coral, fish, sponge, conch and shark are just a few.

Lobster

Lobster Lee came to Key West from North Carolina in 1973 after hearing it was a great place to dive. He worked on shrimp boats for a while and eventually learned all about lobster.

He likes to help out at Lost Reef Dive Shop. Alexis ran into him one day after school when he was waiting for the water taxi. It was good timing, as Alexis' teacher had just assigned the class a project on the lobster and shrimp industries in Key West.

Naja told Alexis she'd collect him from the dive shop in forty-five minutes. That's when the taxi and its passengers would head back to the anchorage.

Sitting in a comfortable, wooden rocking chair, Lobster Lee shared his knowledge of lobster habits with Alexis. He stopped only when divers came in to get their tanks filled, rent equipment, or, to inquire about guided tours.

He told Alexis that there are two ways to catch lobsters. One is in traps and one is by diving for them. Two years ago he took out his diver's license.

"When I get too old to dive," he reflected, "I'll go back to trapping."

Alexis learned that lobster season starts in late summer in August when they begin their migration out of Florida Bay south and west to the Tortugas. In November, when the water gets colder, the lobsters leave. At the end of March, when the water warms up again, the lobsters return. This is opposite to the tourists and part time residents who come to Key West in the cooler months from November to March.

Although no one knows for sure, Lobster Lee believes that lobsters in the waters around Key West begin their journey in

"When I get too old to dive, I'll go back to trapping"

the Caribbean as tiny eggs that float to the algae, sponge, and sea whip communities in Florida Bay. Some are spawned locally and thrive in the mangroves where the soup of the sea nourishes them. At about four and a half months, they circulate to where the waters are warmer and the food source is more adequate and abundant.

Trappers and divers use their knowledge of lobster habits in order to find them. Lobster Lee is up at five in the morning and on the water before the sun comes up. Based on notes that he has kept for over thirty years, he makes multiple dives and looks for patterns in the herd's movement. As social beings, lobsters travel in large numbers.

Lobster Lee examines their feet to get an idea of how long they've been walking and if they've been walking on a soft or hard surface. Their trails are "like

highways under water," he explained. He can also tell by their color where they have been. Lobsters feeding in the mud are white. Those that feed in deep water are brick red. If they feed in shallow water, they are greenish brown. It is illegal to catch undersized lobster. The lobsters caught around the Keys are the right size when they're around fourteen months to two years old.

The phases of the moon affect their location. On the full moon, they "rock up," that is, they hide from predators. On the dark side of the moon, they walk around eating large amounts of food. When Lobster Lee is hunting, he uses a combination of grouper head and cowhide to attract their ravenous appetites. Other things that cause them to move are weather and fishing pressure. In a cold front, they head for deep water. They also know when they are being harassed and are smart enough to know when they need to leave.

From a lobster's point of view

How Divers Catch Lobster

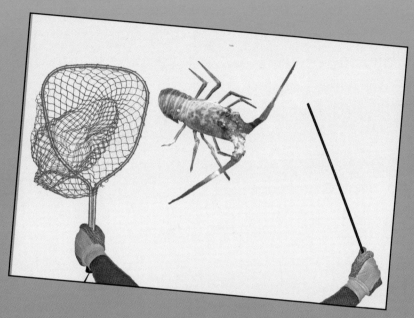

When commercial lobstermen catch lobster, they use large numbers of traps so that they can supply their customers at fish markets and restaurants. Divers catch lobster by hand with only a small net and a tickle stick. The stick is used to reach in the hole where the lobster is hiding and nudge it from behind to make it move outside. Then the diver quickly slips the net over the lobster and back to the boat he swims.

Lobster Lee can stay under water for an hour on a full tank of air. He uses his tickle stick to get the lobster out of his hiding place before putting his net over him. Then he opens the throat, a one way flap on his catch bag, and deposits him where he stays secure while Lobster Lee looks for others. His catch bag can hold around forty pounds or twenty five lobster. When it is full, he gets back on the boat and puts his catch into a well of circulating salt water that keeps the lobsters alive. He changes tanks and goes to another location. Lobster Lee averages around two hundred and fifty pounds a day and eight thousand pounds a year. His customers, the Waterfront Market and the Half Shell Raw Bar, interested only in quality, know that's exactly what they get from Lobster Lee.

Trappers, he explained, require licenses also. Buoys, not only mark traps but their colors reveal who they belong to. Trappers use a square of cowhide as bait.

Sometimes they put a "monkey", which is usually an undersized female, in a trap to attract other lobsters. Lobsters have such a keen sense of smell they will not go into a dirty trap. Every time a trap comes up it has to be scrubbed with a brush and washed with a high pressure hose.

Alexis knew that these creatures went on a lobster walk, but he didn't know where to or for how long. "Do you know where they go?" he asked Lobster Lee.

"Well, for sure they go to the Tortugas. Sometimes they go to the reef and back. Researchers are tracking their movements to find out where else they go," his friend replied.

Naja popped her head around the corner. "Taxi's about to leave, Alexis," she called.

Alexis thanked Lobster Lee who told him to come back tomorrow if he wanted to hear what he knew about shrimp.

A Key West Pink

Shrimp

Alexis did call in to the dive shop the next day, and this is what Lobster Lee told him about shrimp.

Key West Pink is the predominant species of shrimp in the area. They are big and fat, have a great flavor, and are abundant. They spend the day in the mud. At night, they come out to feed.

Shrimp boats go out to the Gulf, north of the Tortugas to drag their nets. With three men on board, they are out for twenty days. Shrimping is hard work. The men tow their nets from sunset till morning. The nets are preceded by a tickle chain that drags along the mud and scoops up the tails of the shrimp. Like lobster, shrimp are very social and travel in large numbers.

Once they get their load on board the shrimpers sort through and throw the by-product catch of towing back into the ocean. The by-product catch comprises fish that are scooped up unintentionally in the nets. Bigger fish learn that when the noise of the motor stops they are in for a good feed.

After they've removed the by-product, the shrimpers sort the shrimp according to size with a tool that looks like a short handled hoe. This process is called culling.

A shrimp boat is like a great floating cooler. After they have been sorted, the shrimp are iced down or placed in brine consisting of ice and salt water.

Coral Reef

The coral reef, seven miles from Key West, is enchanting. It was created by the secretions of tiny animals called coral polyps over thousands of years and is home to many fish species. It is also like a car bumper that absorbs the power of the ocean waves and protects the shorelines. Coral reefs around the world are the only natural formations visible from outer space.

Over the last few decades, concerned citizens have noticed that the reef is crumbling and losing its color. Some say it's because of the tourists walking on it and boats depositing waste carelessly into the water. Others say that the sugar

industry, farms and golf courses on the mainland are depositing nitrogen runoff into Florida Bay. Nitrogen is a fertilizer that causes huge algae blooms to grow and hover over the reef. The problem is that coral needs sunlight for its growth and its beautiful color. If it cannot bathe in sunlight it cannot grow and it becomes dull. Arnaud and Naja have taught their children to care for the environment. When they snorkel at the reef, they are careful not to harm its delicate formations

Captain Jay of the Lucky Fleet has another good day of fishing. The Lucky Charm, Lucky Strike, Lucky Too, and Reel Lucky pass Alexis every day as they make their trips out to the deep water beyond the reef.

or the beautiful fish that live there.

Fishing

Fishing is a popular sport in Key West. Fishermen who don't have their own boats hire charter boats to take them out for

either half a day or a whole day.

Sometimes they cook their catch for dinner. Sometimes they throw it back in the water so the fish can resume life in the sea. Alexis and his dad only fish if they intend to eat what they catch.

Sponges

Once people used sponges exclusively for bathing and cleaning. To meet this huge demand, the locals developed a successful industry harvesting them in the waters around Key West. They scooped them up with rakes, dried them and packaged them off to different parts of the United States.

The Conch is an Amazing Sea Snail

The Conch Shell is the symbol of the Florida Keys. Sometimes people put them outside their houses. In the early days, a conch shell was put outside to announce the birth of a new baby. Today, the conch shell is the mascot for the Key West High School athletic teams. They are known as the Fighting Conchs. This is an interesting thought since the conch is related to the snail. Nevertheless it seems to work as the teams do extremely well at competitions held in the state of Florida.

A quick comparison of the snail and the conch gives you an idea of their similarities and differences. If you've trodden on a snail, you know that its shell is soft and cracks easily. A conch shell, on the other hand, is very hard and crusty. The snail lives mostly on land while the conch lives on the ocean floor. Just like the snail, the conch has been around for about sixty five million years.

The flesh of a snail is a French delicacy known as Escargot. The flesh of the conch is also delicious. It can be cooked and battered but also served raw in a salad with sour orange, lime, salt and pepper, onions and tomato. So many conch have been removed from the ocean floor they are now on the endangered species list in the United States.

If you cut the tip off a conch shell, it becomes a horn. Some people even learn to play it like a musical instrument. Long ago, before they had radios and phones, people used the conch horn to communicate with each other. In the Keys, it announced ships coming into the harbor. Alexis purses his lips, as if he is about to play a trumpet. If he blows hard enough, he can produce a deep sound that will carry to neighboring islands.

Another fascinating thing about the conch shell is that when you hold it up to your ear you can hear the sea. Or, at least, that's how it seems.

Make Your Own Conch Horn

First, saw the tip off the conch shell.

Next, chip out the interior of the hole and file the sharp edges till they're smooth and soft.

Now, take a deep breath, purse your lips, and blow it like a trumpet.

Unfortunately, the sponge population developed a disease which brought an end to the industry. By the time the sponge population recovered, artificial sponges had already been developed and marketed. Nowadays, people use natural sponges for texture painting, bathing and decoration. Alexis found one on the shoreline not far from his boat. "It is really small and incredibly soft," he says. "It stays soft because it's near the sink. Best of all," he adds, "it doesn't smell."

Sharks

Sharks, like the Great White Shark in Jaws, are often portrayed on television as fierce man eaters. Alexis knows that almost all the sharks he might run into around Key West are harmless if left alone. The Nurse Shark, shown below, is sort of like the German Shepherd in your next door neighbor's yard. If you don't bug him, he won't hurt you. The Nurse Shark grows to an average length of six to ten feet and feeds at night on lobster, shrimp, sting ray and other creatures.

While the coral reef is very important ecologically, it has been a heartbreak for some and a gold mine for others.

In the early days, when boats lost their way and washed up on the reef in fierce storms, *WRECK ASHORE!!!!* was a familiar sound in Key West. On hearing the cry, eager settlers raced each other to get to the wreck first.

By salvaging the boat, the wreckers, as they were called, were entitled to a large amount of whatever cargo was on board. Many inhabitants made their fortunes on these wrecks. At one point during this period, Key West became the richest city in Florida.

The first settlers to arrive in Key West were the New England merchants. Then came the Bahamians who had fled to the Bahamas after siding with the British during the American Revolutionary War.

Since there was no lumber on the island, some took their Bahama houses apart and reassembled them in Key West. Likewise, there wasn't much in the way of furniture and dishes so the cargo from wrecked

Captains' walks gave a good view of shipwrecks on the distant reef.

ships wasn't just sold and shipped to other parts of the country, but it was also used to build and support the tiny island.

Some of the early wreckers deliberately moved navigational lights so ships would lose their way. This was illegal and eventually people were hung for it. The Wreckers' Museum on Duval Street provides interesting information about those days.

Alexis' father, Arnaud, is a modern day wrecker salvaging boats washed ashore by hurricanes. He is very good at getting boats off the islands and at lifting them out of the sea. Boat owners pay him for his work but sometimes not as much as the job deserves because he knows some of the people living on the anchorage cannot afford the fee.

Fancy gingerbread designs decorate the old "Conch" houses.

Beautiful mansions were built with the rich salvage.

Many
houses in Key
West have a captain's walk on
top of their roofs. This is where captains
looked out at the conditions of the sea
and observed what was out there. They
are also called widows' walks because this
is where wives whose husbands had been
away
on a long
voyage gazed out at the sea
while waiting for their return.

and their crews raced to their sailboats to be the first to reach the wrecked ship on the reef seven miles away. The captain who reached the wreck first was in charge of the salvage and could claim the biggest share of the prize.

Today, the race to the reef is re-enacted each year with all boats in the harbor trying to show off their boats' speed. Their prize is no longer rich salvaged cargo but the right to brag about having the fastest boat in Key West.

The Great Wreckers' Race

When the call 'Wreck Ashore' was sounded in old Key West, captains

In this rich environment of land and sea, Alexis has been inspired, since the age of five, to write poetry and stories, as well as draw colorful pictures of his ideas. In so doing, he is understanding and representing the abundant, soulful and exciting world around him.

Alexis is in good company, for many creative people, not just artists and writers, but also musicians, dancers and actors, nurture the longings of their imaginations here.

What is it about this tropical paradise that allows such creative voice? Is it the fact that Key West is a tiny island in the Atlantic Ocean where palm trees sway and the water reflects in brilliant jade? Is it just

that living by the water provides a sense of freedom and endless possibility?

Is it that similar minded people are drawn here and encourage each other in their journeys of productivity and

Many Key West homes have Mario Sanchez paintings on their walls.

contentment?

Perhaps it's the preference of Key Westers to travel under their own power. Walking, riding bicycles, and sailing rather than driving, not only produces less pollution but possibly unclutters the mind.

The artist, Mario Sanchez, was born in Key West. The writer, Ernest Hemingway, made Key West his home, and so did the singer and songwriter, Jimmy Buffet.

Mario Sanchez

Mario Sanchez, a Cuban-American folk artist, was born in Key West in 1908. He spent his whole life here until he died recently. He began work when he was twelve years old shining shoes from a stand beside his father's coffee shop. At a very early age, he began to observe the local characters and their work. When he was older, he worked as a janitor at a gallery that would later exhibit his art.

During Mario's youth, Key West was famous for it's cigar manufacturing industry. While the workers rolled tobacco leaves into cigars, Mario read to them about local events from the newspaper. This helped to pass the time for the workers, who, in a factory environment, could easily become bored. Mario depicted this, and other neighborhood events and people, in woodcuts that he then painted. Often he painted under a sprawling sapodilla tree in his backyard. Prints of his work can be purchased locally.

During Mario's youth, Key West was famous for its cigar manufacturing industry.

Alexis has studied Mario's art in school and likes the way he uses shapes and color.

Mario's workshop was under a sapodilla tree in his backyard. Here he recreated beautiful scenes from his childhood such as this cigar factory where Mario once worked as a "reader".

56

Ernest Hemingway

Ernest Hemingway was a famous war hero, fisherman and author. Visitors love to take a tour through his house to learn more about his life and times and to see the office where he wrote. An interesting feature about his house is the fifty or so cats that live there. Some bear the peculiar feature of having six toes.

Two of his famous novels are "A Farewell to Arms" depicting his war experience, and, "The Old Man and the Sea" about an old Cuban fisherman who displays quiet courage and dignity battling a huge fish far out at sea in a tiny boat.

Key West celebrates his life in July during a week of planned events called Hemingway Days. One of the most popular events is the Hemingway look alike contest held at Sloppy Joe's.

Hemingway lived in this house on Whitehead Street from 1930 to 1938 where he wrote "A Farewell to Arms" and other famous books.

Some of the fifty cats at the Hemingway House have six toes instead of five.

Tennessee Williams was a well known writer who lived in this Key West house. He wrote famous plays like "Cat on a Hot Tin Roof".

Jimmy Buffet

Jimmy Buffet has written many popular songs about life in Key West. One of the favorites is "Cheeseburger in Paradise".

His songs inspired many people to move to Key West and themselves experience the relaxed lifestyle of boiling shrimp for dinner and sailing on summer breezes.

9. The Story of the Conch Republic
(or We Seceded Where Others Failed)

Royalty of the Conch Republic
Past and Present

Secretary General

Queen Barbie

Fairy Princess

**General Jeff and the
Lady Ain't Waiting**

King Mel

The Great Sea Battle

Besides artists and writers, Key West has attracted others who are not afraid to make a statement. In 1982, the Federal Government set up a roadblock on US Highway 1. This slowed traffic considerably as it is the only road through the Florida Keys to Key West.

Every vehicle, going and coming, was checked for narcotics and people who were living in the country illegally. This put a serious curb on tourism and also detained residents.

Claiming that it was like a border patrol dividing foreign countries, Mayor Dennis Wardlow and the local council of Key West decided to officially break away from the United States.

War was declared but they surrendered after one minute and demanded foreign aid. From then on the Keys became known as the Conch Republic. Their motto is "We Seceded Where Others Failed." The people are proud of being the "World's First Fifth World Nation" seeking to bring more humor, warmth and respect to the world. The conch shell is their proud emblem.

The Conch Republic inaugurated a King and a Queen. A Secretary General issues passports and welcomes visitors to his office. Although a Conch Republic passport is not a valid document, travelers, nevertheless, use it from time to time.

Key West characters have always been colorful starting with the pirates who occasionally visited the island to obtain water.

Other official dignitaries include a General, an Admiral, a Lady Ain't Waiting, and a Fairy Princess. They have the important job of representing the Conch Republic in parades and at other official functions.

Every year the city of Key West celebrates its staged secession from the United States with many events, one of which is "The Great Sea Battle." Residents and tourists alike, often wearing raincoats, either man boats or take up their positions on the dock at Mallory Square.

The battle begins as both sides attack each other with squishy, old tomatoes, eggs and water cannons. The huge play fight ends when the troops become tired after their fierce battle and decide to go home. It is a fine example of how the people of Key West love to have fun.

This year, Arnaud, Naja and Clementine fired their water cannons from the taxi while Alexis shot back at them with tomatoes from the dock.

Western Union
Flagship of the Conch Republic Navy

HURRICANES

ARE SCARY

10.

When Alexis was a baby, Hurricane Georges headed for the Florida Keys. Fearing their boats would not survive, Arnaud sailed the family up Florida Bay to the Shark River in the swamp land known as the Everglades. This desolate and forbidding area is home to alligators and mosquitoes as well as flocks of egrets, storks, cormorants, blue herons, cranes, seagulls, frigate birds and osprey. The fish that fill the streams feed the birds and alligators. People have tried to settle there but the endless wetness and soft ground have eventually driven them out. Anyone who has camped in the Everglades knows it's easy to get lost in its complex twists and turns.

A chilling story about a sugar cane plantation owner named Watson haunts these swamps. Every so often he went to town to get supplies from the general store and to hire help. Residents of Chokoloskee became suspicious when the hired help were never seen again. When Watson was confronted with their murders, he blamed the deaths on his foreman and shot him. Watson thought he had gotten away with it, but the next time he came to town a dozen or so residents opened fire on him. With Watson out of the way, people stopped disappearing.

Despite the Everglade's chilling folk history and its hostile environment, Arnaud knew that the dense mangrove roots would cushion his boats through high winds. He also knew that the forty foot mangroves would prevent crashing waves from reaching the boats and tossing them around.

So in this natural setting that offered a

Facts About Hurricanes

Nothing strikes fear into the hearts of boaters and people who live along the ocean than the cry, "Hurricane Coming". Every minute counts in the rush to protect property on the land and water and then move to higher ground.

These storms usually start out as something much more innocent and far away. When the winds first begin revolving in a counterclockwise direction, the weather condition is known as a tropical depression. As the winds reach 33 knots (equal to 39 miles per hour), the weather pattern is called a tropical storm and is given a special name like 'Dennis' or 'Katrina'. The winds are actually spiralling inward towards an "eye" which has low pressure and is therefore sucking the air towards it. The weather within the eye is very calm, un-

like the terrible storm swirling around it.

As the storm's winds grow above 64 knots (or 74 miles per hour), it is now classified as a Category 1 hurricane. At this level, most homes would be safe when it came ashore, but if it grows all the way to the most feared Category 5 hurricane, its winds of more than 155 miles per hour will destroy many houses. Sailors know that if they stand facing the wind the center of the hurricane is in a direction just behind their right shoulder.

In the northern hemisphere, the counterclockwise rotating hurricane curves slightly to the right as it moves forward. The forward velocity combined with the rotating winds makes the right side of the hurricane the most dangerous. Here a boat or a house will feel the greatest wind force.

ESCAPE TO

Gaspard enters the Shark River as it escapes from Hurricane Georges

safe
haven,
they waited
while a force that
could destroy them passed
over. They had no idea when
they were out of danger. Eventually
Arnaud climbed to the top of the eighty
five foot mast so he could pick up a signal
for his cell phone. When he learned from
friends that Georges had moved further
up the mainland, he sailed his boat and
his family safely back home to Key West.

Usually Key West residents, both on
land and sea, have sufficient warning
about the threat of tropical storms in
the Atlantic Ocean developing into

SHARK RIVER

Coco Loco lies tied up to a nice mangrove cushion

people, cars or houses. Those who live on boats secure their homes too.

Arnaud has very heavy anchors that are secured onto long, thick ropes or chains about five to ten times as long as the depth of water under the boat. Sometimes he uses two anchors in opposite directions in what is called a Bahamian mooring. Not only is he safer

hurricanes. Those who live in houses cover their windows and doors with boards or steel shutters and take everything indoors that could fly around and crash into

by having a second anchor, but, as the wind circles from different directions, the boat as it turns into the wind, is held in one spot. Sometimes sailors will sink a huge mooring weight made of concrete or steel into the sand in the hope that it will not drag.

Usually Arnaud stays onboard so he can maneuver his boat if he needs to. Naja takes Alexis and Clementine to a hotel where they wait with other friends from their neighborhood until the winds die down, the cutting rain stops and it is safe to return home.

Hurricane Katrina took Key West by surprise. Everyone thought she was headed north towards Ft. Lauderdale, but then she suddenly turned south. The winds picked up speed and screamed through the trees. About ten thirty at night the water heaved in huge valleys and mountains. Such waves made it too difficult to take the water taxi to shore so Alexis and his family were stuck on the boat.

When Arnaud saw, through the blinding rain, a large boat free of its mooring, heading towards him like a playground bully, he turned on the motor and maneuvered the boat around to avoid being hit. Then he noticed other vessels not securely anchored and spent the whole night steering away from boats that could crash into his family's home.

The roller coaster waves turned their stomachs and every member of the family made at least two visits to the head. Arnaud is a good sailor and a smart captain so he was able to save his family and his home. Others, that night, were

Arnaud knew that the dense mangrove roots would cushion his boats.

not so lucky. Two days later the anchorage was a graveyard of broken boats and dangling masts. Some were turned upside down after smashing onto the shore of Christmas Tree Island.

After a hurricane, if their roof hasn't blown off or their house hasn't flooded, people on land clean up fallen leaves and branches and take down the shutters and boards. On the boat, they put back the sails, canvas, nets, cushions, ropes, lines and other things they usually keep outside.

Hurricanes have sunk many ships in the waters around Key West. Perhaps the most famous is the Spanish galleon, the Nuestra Senora de Atocha.

Some boats ran out of luck during Katrina.

The Story of the Nuestra Senora de Atocha

The famous Spanish explorer, Christopher Columbus, discovered the New World in 1492. Shortly afterwards, the Spanish Empire spread into the Caribbean and South America. There the Spaniards gathered silver from the mines in Potosi, gold and emeralds from Columbia and pearls from Venezuela. They collected more gold from Mexico as well as silk, porcelain and fine china from the Philippines.

Several Spanish fleets gathered up this vast treasure from all the ports in the New World each year. They usually came together in Havana in July to make the long and perilous sail back to Spain with their cache known as the "Treasure of the Indies."

The Nuestro Senora de Atocha was attached to the Tierre Firma Fleet. She was a command galleon, an almiranta, which proudly displayed twenty bronze cannons. Her job was to defend the fleet from the rear against pirates and English warships wanting to plunder the fleet's incredible treasures. She was such a prestigious, comfortable and secure ship that forty-eight merchants, nobility and government officials chose to voyage with her on the 1622 return trip to Spain. As well as a large number of passengers and their personal riches, the Atocha was greatly overloaded, that year, with a huge cargo of gold, silver, copper, indigo and tobacco bales.

The combined Tierra Firma fleet of twenty eight ships finally left Havana Sunday, September 4, 1622 after numerous delays caused it to set sail six weeks late. Safely offshore, the fleet tacked to the east, then to the north to get into the Gulf Stream which would carry the ships to Spain. However, when they reached the Gulf Stream early Monday morning, they were greeted by fierce winds that tossed them around like toys. Many of the crewmen and passengers became sick with the relentless up and down, side to side pounding the boats endured. By Monday evening, the wild winds and churning sea had completely broken up the fleet. Each ship was alone to battle the first hurricane of the season which they now knew they had sailed into. Early Tuesday morning the Atocha's mainmast broke. Crewmen tried desperately to drop anchor but the wind dragged the ship anyway. Waves lifted the Atocha high, then dropped it again in a trough of shallow water. The last bullying heave smashed the Atocha down hard on the jutting reef. Amidst desperate screams the hatch was opened. People clung to whatever they could until the force of the water swept them through the surging seas. Two hundred and sixty noblemen and crew drowned.

Amazingly, a seaman, two teenage

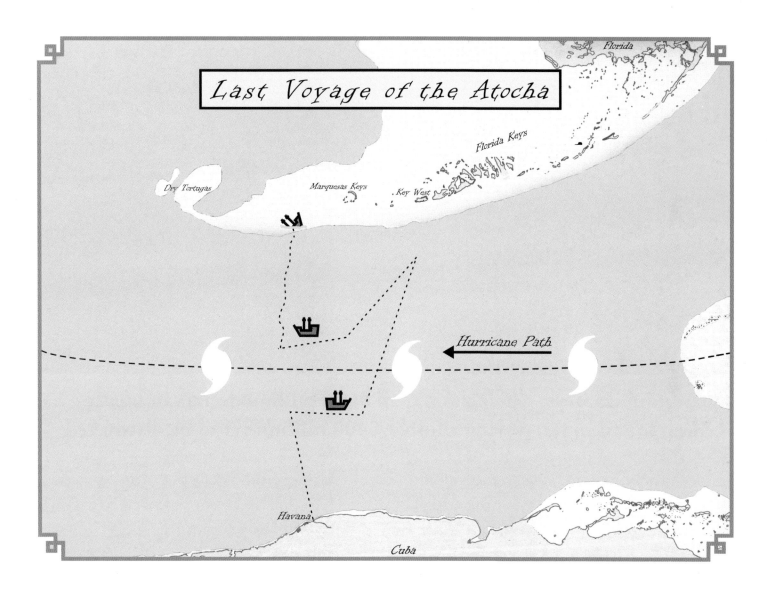

Last Voyage of the Atocha

Florida

Florida Keys

Dry Tortugas

Marquesas Keys

Key West

Hurricane Path

Havana

Cuba

apprentices and two black slaves survived because they had tied themselves to the rigging of the mizzenmast. Weakened and almost blinded by the sun, they were eventually rescued by a launch from the merchant ship, Santa Cruz.

The Marquesas Keys, where more than $600 million dollars in treasure has been found so far, leaving another $400 million yet to be discovered

Besides immense gold, silver, emerald and pearl treasure, also buried with the Atocha was seventeenth century Spanish history in the stories and belongings of those who perished.

The surviving ships limped back to Havana. The Marquis de Cadereita called a meeting of the fleet's pilots and asked if they should still try to sail back to Spain or wait until next year. The consensus was that they should delay the return voyage and concentrate on the recovery of the Atocha's treasure. Two other missing galleons, the Margarita and the Rosario, were also burying treasure on the sandy sea bottom with each passing day.

Ten days later the most experienced captain, Caspar de Vargas, headed back to the Keys with five vessels. He and his crew located the Atocha. However, the second hurricane of the season, which hit October 5, just one month after the first, destroyed their efforts. Once again the heavy seas lashed at the Atocha. This time her hull was ripped open and her heavy cannons flung for miles. The lower hull sank to the murky bottom in fifty six feet of water. After clinging to each other on land in order to save their own lives, Caspar de Vargas and his search party were unable to relocate the original site of the sunken Atocha. The Spanish never

John Brandon displays the treasure he and other divers discovered in 1985

recovered their treasure.

When Mel Fisher was eleven years old, he created a hard hat diver's suit to explore the murky waters of a lagoon near his house in Indiana. His dream was to one day go from exploring lagoons to exploring oceans. Mel, a musician and engineer, opened his own scuba dive shop in California and became interested in searching for sunken treasure. Discovering the site of the Atocha became his goal. After sixteen years of researching, planning and saying every morning, "Today's the day!" he finally succeeded.

On July 20, 1985, his divers, operating from a vessel called, "Dauntless", discovered the first gold bars, 363 years after Caspar de Vargas had failed.

Don Kincaid, a photographer and diver brought up the first gold chain. He took the picture, that appears on the previous page, of his friend with newly discovered treasure. Mel Fisher and his team would go on to salvage, from this underwater archeological site, millions of dollars worth of gold and silver bars, silver coins, called pieces of eight in English but reales in Spanish, and, gold coins, called doubloons in English but escuda in Spanish. Emeralds, gold chains, copper bars, jewel-encrusted brooches and necklaces, were other examples of precious treasure. Salvaged olive jars called ollas jars that preserved meats, fruits and vegetables for the voyage, gun like weapons called arquebus and swords, and beautifully crafted food utensils were just some of the artifacts that shed light on Spanish history in the seventeenth century.

Mel opened up museums where the public could share in his journey and observe the treasure. Alexis loves to visit the Mel

"Today's the day!"

Fisher Museum in Key West. His friend, Cory, a scientist and diver, discusses with him the latest finds and explains how they are bathed in a solution to gently remove the encrustation caused by centuries under the sea. Cory also explains how gold does not become encrusted. Unlike silver, it remains as shiny as the day it sank to the bottom of the ocean.

In tribute to his indomitable spirit, Mel Fisher was declared the permanent king of the Conch Republic.

The early Spanish cannons looked much different from the ones we now associate with sailing ships in the Caribbean. It must be remembered that the Spanish ruled islands like Cuba for over four hundred years and there were great improvements in ships and weapons from the early Columbus days.

Many of the items recovered from the Atocha gave researchers insights into everyday life of the early Spaniards such as this tiny pair of scissors found in the wreckage.

Alexis ponders parts of an arquebus that once belonged to a Spanish conquistador drowned on the Atocha.

Treasures of the New World

Silver Pieces of Eight

One Half Real

One Real

Two Reales

Four Reales

Eight Reales

Gold Doubloons

One Half Escuda

One Escuda

Two Escuda

Four Escuda

Eight Escuda

Emeralds

Precious stones, like emeralds, were also part of the treasure discovered in the New World.

Pearls

Pearls came from the Atlantic Pearl Oyster which can still be found around Key West.

The Spanish mined gold and silver in the new world and shipped coins and ingots back on galleons like the Atocha.

Currents in the Ocean

After the Spanish discovered America and began making frequent trips in their large galleons, they soon realized that there were strong currents flowing in the oceans.

A current that we call the Gulfstream flows by the northern shore of Cuba, around the Florida peninsula and across the north Atlantic toward Europe. In some places this current can flow as much as four miles per hour which greatly helped a large galleon possibly only making seven or eight miles per hour. As the Gulfstream nears Europe, southern moving currents flow past the Canary Islands down to the Azores and join the South Equatorial currents heading westward back to the Caribbean Sea.

If Alexis were to put a note in a bottle and drop it in the Gulfstream near Key West, it might be carried to Ireland, England, Sweden, France, Portugal, Spain, Africa, or any of the island groups in the Atlantic or Caribbean. Or it might just make endless circles around the Atlantic for years. Maybe he would receive a letter from a boy or girl who found the bottle and replied before dropping it back in the ocean.

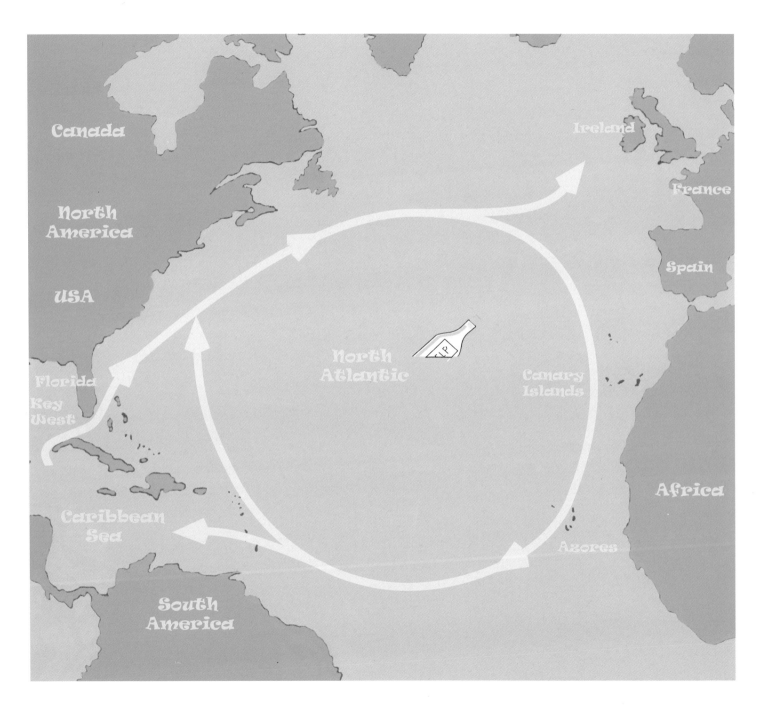

Mallory Square comes alive as the sun prepares to lay rest on another day in Paradise. A couple of hours before sunset, street performers set up their props and equipment. Vendors lay out their homemade creations on various sizes of tables. It's like a fair complete with popcorn and lemonade.

Enormous cruise ships, docked a few yards away, stand watch as their passengers stroll along the waterfront soaking in the end of the day.

The sun lowers on the horizon. Tightrope walkers, musicians, tumblers, fire jugglers, dogs and cats entertain the crowds. Finally, but very quickly, the sun sinks below the water. Observers hope to see a green flash that might occur right after it disappears, but that is rare.

The Cat Man, Dominique, is a friend of Alexis'. He is from France, just like Alexis' Dad, so they speak French together whenever they meet.

Oscar, a beautiful cat with shiny, black fur thrills the audience when he leaps through a hoop of fire. An array of tabby, smoky grey, black and white cats

Dominique and his amazing cat show

roll, leap and walk across the tightrope stretched between two high, red stools. While he coaxes the cats to do what he wants, Dominique pulls funny faces, contorts his body and cavorts in front of the crowd. At the end of the show, he passes around a bag for the crowd's offering. It's kind of like buying a ticket after the performance and deciding how much to pay.

Although sunset, like sunrise, is a predictable event, witnessing the sky's transformation from light to dark is an acknowledgement of the awesomeness of our world.

Performers of every age try to please the crowd.

Losing Your Home

Even though technology can provide detailed information about potential disasters and humans can make the best preparations, nature will ultimately have the final say.

While still recovering from the effects of three hurricanes, Dennis, Rita and Katrina, in the same year, Key West and the Florida Keys braced themselves for yet a fourth. Her name was Wilma. As land residents made preparations to secure their homes and belongings, Arnaud and his neighbors on the anchorage began, once again, clearing the decks and sinking heavy anchors.

Wilma's winds raged as she passed close to the Keys ripping off roofs and upheaving trees. The salt water from the five foot tidal surge rushed through people's houses and destroyed everything it touched. In its wake it left a trail of broken dreams.

As soon as he could, Arnaud motored the water taxi out to the anchorage. What he saw filled him with a profound sense of loss. Both Gaspard and Coco Loco were gone. Two days later, he found Gaspard flung north onto Fleming Key. After an extensive search, he accepted that he would never find Coco Loco. Along with their home, Alexis and Clementine lost their toys and collections of favorite things. Three hundred copies of the poetry books Alexis sells at Blue Heaven also sank to the bottom of the ocean.

From time to time, the family is reminded of Coco Loco. Naja found the roof of the aft deck washed up on Christmas Tree Island. A couple of weeks later they saw a friend transporting a teak table in his dinghy. When they looked closer, they realized it was from their sunken home and got it back.

Alexis and his family are still in the process of rebuilding their life on the anchorage. Arnaud bought a new boat for them to live on for now. Although they have lost many personal treasures, they still have each other. Arnaud and Naja are teaching their children much about resiliency and what is important. They will continue to live in the waters just off Key West where anything is possible. In fact, Alexis doesn't see himself leaving Paradise. "Why would I?" he says. "Everything I need is right here."

...But those who just drift upon the water
  Waiting to find something else
  Shall discover the wonders and magnificence
  Of the Worshiped Island...

from The Worshiped Island
by Alexis Girard D'Albissin